FIGHTING FORCES IN THE AIR

HH-60 PAVE HAWK

LYNN STONE

Rourke

Publishing LLC
Vero Beach, Florida 32964

www.rourkepublishing.com

PHOTO CREDITS: All photos courtesy of the U.S. Air Force

Title page: *The Pave Hawk's main job is to conduct rescue operations in hostile environments.*

Editor: Frank Sloan

Library of Congress Cataloging-in-Publication Data

Stone, Lynn M.
  HH-60 Pave Hawk / Lynn M. Stone.
      p. cm. -- (Fighting forces in the air)
  Includes bibliographical references and index.
  ISBN 1-59515-184-2 (hardcover)
  1. Pave Hawk (Search and rescue helicopter) 2. United States. Air Force--
Search and rescue operations. I. Title.
  II. Series: Stone, Lynn M. Fighting forces in the air.
  UG1232.S43S76 2004
  623.74'66--dc22
                                        2004011747

Printed in the USA

CG/CG

TABLE OF CONTENTS

THE HH-60 PAVE HAWK

The HH-60 Pave Hawk is a military helicopter flown by the United States Air Force, primarily for search-and-rescue operations in combat conditions. The Pave Hawk is one of several "Hawk" helicopters in U.S. military service. The Pave "Hawk" is a twin-engine, medium-lift helicopter. It's a highly **modified** version of the U.S. Army's UH-60 Black Hawk helicopter. A helicopter with a similar name, the Air Force's MH-53J/M Pave Low, is a larger, heavy-lift helicopter.

A Pave Hawk flies on a mission after refueling from an HC-130P Combat Shadow aircraft.

▲

Hovering just 6 feet (1.8 m) above the waves, a Pave Hawk and its skilled pilot practice a sea rescue.

The Pave Hawk is a highly **versatile** machine—It can do many different things well. One of its greatest assets is its ability to **hover**—to remain in flight in one place above the ground, like a bumblebee or hummingbird. Another asset is its ability to land and take off on a very small plot of ground, even somewhat rough ground. Helicopters lift off like birds flying off a branch; a helicopter doesn't need to taxi and build up speed before becoming airborne. Its broad, overhead rotor blade provides enough lift to take a helicopter straight up.

HH-60G Characteristics

Function: combat search and
   rescue helicopter
Builder: United
   Technologies/Sikorsky
   Aircraft Company
Power Source: Two General
   Electric T700-GE-700 or
   T700-GE-701C engines
Thrust: 1,560 – 1,940 shaft
   horsepower, each engine
Length: 64 feet, 8 inches
   (17.1 meters)
Height: 16 feet, 8 inches
   (4.4 meters)
Rotor Diameter: 53 feet,
   7 inches (14.1 meters)
Speed: 184 miles per hour
   (294 kilometers per hour)
Maximum Takeoff Weight:
   22,000 pounds
   (9,900 kilograms)
Range: 580 miles
   (928 kilometers)
Crew: Four (two pilots, one
   flight engineer, one gunner)
Date Deployed: 1982

Because of these advantages and others, the Pave Hawk can be sent into difficult and dangerous areas. On a search-and-rescue mission, a Pave Hawk crew will look for and attempt to rescue people. These may be Air Force crews whose planes have been shot down.

The Pave Hawk can carry eight to ten soldiers along with its normal crew of four. Pave Hawks often transport soldiers being sent on special assignments behind enemy lines. After dropping the soldiers, the Pave Hawk can slip away in low-altitude flight and later return to pick them up.

FACT FILE ★

BY FLYING AT LOW ALTITUDES, A PAVE HAWK IS DIFFICULT TO SPOT UNTIL IT IS ALMOST AT ITS DESTINATION.

▲ *A Pave Hawk hovers over the U.S. Embassy in Liberia where the helicopter was part of a humanitarian assistance-and-rescue operation.*

Specially trained and equipped Pave Hawk flight crews can perform night operations. A Night Vision Goggle (NVG) system is one of the crew's basic tools. Night goggles worn by the crew use **infrared** technology to make objects that would otherwise be invisible become visible.

Pave Hawks can operate day or night and in poor, although not all, weather conditions. Once at its flying destination, a Pave Hawk can leave— or pick up—soldiers by a variety of means. The easiest way, of course, is by landing. But if a landing site is unavailable, the Pave Hawk can use a rope ladder or hoist. Its 200-foot- (61-m-) long cable hoist can lift 600 pounds (270 kg) from a surface to the helicopter. The hoist can lift three people at the same time or one patient on a litter.

▲ Two HH-60s provide cover for pararescuemen practicing the rescue of a downed pilot.

Pararescuemen unhook the hoist of a Pave Hawk.

Sometimes the Pave Hawk crews use other methods for inserting or extracting combat soldiers. It can drop soldiers with parachutes. Another option is to have soldiers **rappel** down a rope or use other roping techniques to reach the ground.

A Pave Hawk can also place soldiers onto a ship by using one or more rope techniques. A Pave Hawk can lower a rubber raft, a crew for the raft, and finally a raft engine.

▲ *Rain doesn't prevent Marines from boarding this HH-60 for a mission out of Sierra Leone.*

◀ *Pave Hawk pararescue crews practice many kinds of rope hoist operations.*

In addition to combat missions, Pave Hawks are used for non-military purposes, such as search and rescue. They can airlift sick or injured people in emergencies and help provide relief supplies, when disasters occur. Pave Hawks work on anti-drug operations, too, and support NASA space shuttle operations.

The Pave Hawk has a cargo hook that will carry an 8,000-pound (3,629-kg) load outside the aircraft.

A pararescueman prepares to rappel from a Pave Hawk in Iraq. ▶

◀

While one airman steadies a 15-foot- (4.6-m-) long ladder, a fellow pararescueman climbs into an HH-60 in West Africa.

▲

The pilot of an HH-60G prepares to launch a mission during Operation Iraqi Freedom.

CHAPTER TWO

FLYING THE PAVE HAWK

A Pave Hawk normally flies with a crew of four—two pilots, a flight engineer, and a gunner. It has two engines and a top speed of 184 miles per hour (294 km/h). Its normal range—the distance it can fly without refueling—is 580 miles (928 km).

All Pave Hawks have automatic flight control systems, color all-weather radar, and a system to keep their rotor blades ice-free. The rotor blades fold, making the Pave Hawk much easier to transport by ship or cargo aircraft.

FACT FILE ★

THE PAVE HAWK CAN BE REFUELED IN MID-AIR THROUGH A SPECIAL TUBE, THUS EXTENDING ITS RANGE.

CHAPTER THREE

PAVE HAWK EQUIPMENT

Pave Hawks are equipped with a variety of new electronics flight systems, like Forward Looking Infrared (FLIR). FLIR improves a pilot's night vision. FLIR systems measure infrared heat energy that objects release naturally. Infrared heat energy is invisible except through special instruments.

▲ *Air crews load an HH-60 aboard a C-17 cargo plane for transport to a combat zone.*

▲ *Special equipment allows Pave Hawks to be "night hawks."*

FLIR can detect infrared energy and create images from it—even in total darkness! FLIR doesn't produce a perfect image. But it does produce a reasonably clear image. A user can distinguish between such objects as trees, trucks, and soldiers.

▲ *A Pave Hawk gunner inspects his GAU-II mini gun.*

For combat operations, Pave Hawks are equipped with two 7.62mm machine guns. For defense they have a radar warning receiver and an infrared jammer. A jammer sends signals that confuse an enemy's infrared equipment. Pave Hawks also carry **chaff**. Chaff consists of metal strips for release into the air. The metal strips confuse enemy radar.

FACT FILE ★

THE PAVE HAWKS CARRY FLARES. THEIR HEAT CAN LURE AN ENEMY'S HEAT-SEEKING MISSILE AWAY FROM THE PAVE HAWK.

▲ *One of the new HH-60H Pave Hawks flies a reconnaissance mission over Baghdad, Iraq.*

In 2003, the Air Force began an update of Pave Hawks. Plans were to upgrade 49 of the 105 Pave Hawks owned by the Air Force by 2007. The "new" HH-60Gs were to be fitted with what is known as the Block 152 upgrade package. It features improved communication and navigation systems. It also has a new **countermeasure** system to combat enemy missile, laser, and radar threats. Overall, Block 152 should make flying easier and safer for Pave Hawk crews.

A new, outside gun mount system on the upgraded HH-60s will feature a .50 caliber machine gun in addition to the existing guns. The new gun is positioned so that it can be triggered by the pilot.

CHAPTER FOUR

The Hawk helicopters were developed in the 1970s and built by Sikorsky Aviation, now a part of United Technologies. The first Pave Hawk models were **deployed** for service in 1982.

Sikorsky has built several Hawk-family helicopters with such names as Seahawk, Knight Hawk, Jay Hawk, Night Hawk, and Black Hawk.

▲ *Another one of the "Hawks," this Navy Sea Hawk flies as part of an anti-submarine squadron.*

▲ *Pave Hawk helicopters prepare to take off on a mission In Iraq during Operation Iraqi Freedom.*

In 1991, during Operation Desert Storm, Pave Hawks flew combat search-and-rescue missions in Iraq, Saudi Arabia, Kuwait, and elsewhere around the Persian Gulf. They also flew emergency evacuations for U.S. Navy SEAL (SEa, Air, and Land) Special Forces teams.

▲ *This HH-60G Pave Hawk is at a base in Sierra Leone where it can depart for emergency evacuations elsewhere.*

In 1999, Pave Hawks flew to support NATO (North Atlantic Treaty Organization) forces engaged in combat operations over Yugoslavia during Operation Allied Force. During OAF, Pave Hawks rescued two U.S. Air Force pilots from behind enemy lines.

In March, 2000, three Pave Hawks were sent to Mozambique. They supported international flood relief operations by delivering more than 160 tons (145 metric tons) of relief supplies.

FACT FILE ★

Sixteen Pave Hawks were deployed in 2003 as part of the American force in Operation Iraqi Freedom.

▲

During the next few years, some Pave Hawks will be retired. Newer models will be equipped with the latest flight systems and continue in service.

CHAPTER FIVE

FLYING INTO THE FUTURE

The oldest HH-60Gs are nearing the end of their service lives. Like any aircraft, HH-60Gs are subject to increasing mechanical and structural problems with age. Studies by the Air Force will determine whether to extend their lives with major overhauls or to seek new aircraft for combat search and rescue.

Meanwhile, newer Pave Hawks are undergoing upgrades. These helicopters are likely to remain in active service well into the second decade of the century.

Glossary

chaff (CHAFF) — small metal strips released into the air to confuse radar systems

countermeasure (KAUNT ur MEZH ur) — a strategy or system used to avoid being struck by enemy fire

deployed (dih PLOYD) — to have been placed into a chosen position for possible military use

hover (HUV ur) — to remain in mid-air over one small surface area without moving forward, backward, up, or down

infrared (IN fruh RED) — (also known as *thermal radiation* or *infrared rays*) the invisible-to-the-naked-eye energy rays given off by any warm object, such as a human being, battle tank, or airplane; invisible heat rays that can be detected by special instruments

modified (MOD uh FYED) — changed in some way from the original

rappel (ruh PEL) — to maneuver down a rope

versatile (VURS uh tul) — able to perform many tasks or skills

INDEX

FURTHER READING

Schleifer, Jay. *Combat Helicopters*. Capstone, 1996

Sweetman, Bill. *Combat Rescue Helicopters: The MH-53 Pave Lows*. Capstone, 2002

Sweetman, Bill. *Attack Helicopters: The AH-64 Apaches*. Capstone, 2001

WEBSITES TO VISIT

www.globalsecurity.org/military/systems/aircraft/hh-60g.htm
www.af.mil/factsheets

ABOUT THE AUTHOR

Lynn M. Stone is the author of more than 400 children's books. He is a talented natural history photographer as well. Lynn, a former teacher, travels worldwide to photograph wildlife in its natural habitat.